MiniScript Shorthand

An easy alternative to traditional systems

TABLE OF CONTENTS

Introduction

Existing shorthand systems provide non-alphabetical symbols or outlines for words and common phrases to write them in a short form and increase the writing speed. A number of writing strokes is significantly reduced and a high speed can be attained.

However, a great deal of time must be spent on memorization using such systems and retention is difficult unless you practice writing the outlines on a daily basis.

On the other hand, speedwriting methods use alphabet letters and are easier to learn. But they require two or three strokes to write a standard letter and can not match a writing speed attainable by non-alphabetical shorthand.

Usually, all existing speedwriting and shorthand methods are based on assigning a unique outline or code to an individual word and memorizing a large number of abbreviations is a very lengthy process.

It is unlikely that you will use regularly all the codes or outlines memorized. Those that are not used daily are forgotten and cannot be remembered when needed, so proficiency declines. In addition, you might to have to create your own codes or outlines for specific words related to your vocabulary.

Computer programs could potentially reduce the difficulties transcribing large volumes of symbols. But memorization of a unique code for every word is a 'catch 22' problem. In order for the computer software produce a full word the user must know the corresponding abbreviation.

MiniScript Concept

The MiniScript system is an alternative that combines both the simplicity of speedwriting and a high writing speed of non-alphabetical shorthand. MiniScript employs: a) a proven and popular EasyScript alphabet-based abbreviation methodology that reduces considerably the memorization volume by using a small set of abbreviating rules and b) writing actual abbreviations with special symbols to attain writing speeds comparable to non-alphabetical shorthand.

If MiniScript forms are created using EasyScript method and positionally placed symbols you will need to remember only a list of 9 special characters representing a full English alphabet. To reduce the memorization one symbol is used to write three letters. For instance, letters A, B and C are written using '.' by placing it on the top, middle and bottom line positions.

Example: A ˙   B ·   C .

As a result, this combined approach of using EasyScript method and a small set of non-alphabetical will enable you to increase your writing speed compared to alphabet-based systems.

To achieve a high writing speed and process spoken information effectively at the speed it is generated any MiniScript abbreviation should not exceed more than three symbols per word.

As described above, MiniScript consists of two components: 1) EasyScript (ES) alphabet-based abbreviation methodology that reduces considerably the memorization volume by using a small set of abbreviating rules and 2) writing actual abbreviations with special symbols to attain writing speeds comparable to non-alphabetical shorthand.

Consequently, mastering MiniScript is a two-step process consisting of: 1) studying EasyScript abbreviation method and 2) learning how to write EasyScript abbreviations with non-alphabetical special symbols assigned to represent an individual alphabet letter. Special symbols from the conventional QWERTY keyboard are used which are familiar to any person using a computer and require little or no training.

Each lesson consists of two sections to study both alphabetical and symbol forms separately for the same set of words. Two practice exercises within each section are offered. The first exercise shows the practice words and corresponding alphabetical or symbol forms. The second exercise has only the practice words and you need to write the appropriate abbreviations and symbols memorized from the first exercise.

Transcription Software

ComputerScript (CS) software allows entering of EasyScript alphabetical abbreviations using conventional QWERTY keyboard and provides automatic transcription into readable form. The CS software runs on WINDOWS XP or higher platforms. For more information call: **617-527-4988** or visit our website: WWW.EASYSCRIPT.COM.

We are considering in the near future developing software to transcribe the MiniScript symbol forms into readable format.

On-Site Training and Licensing

Legend Co. offers training programs custom tailored to your group (any size) at a time and location that is convenient to you. Also, site licenses are available for this training to be conducted by your staff. This course is also available in a classroom format for teaching middle/high school and college students.

Here is a sample of Fortune 500 companies, government agencies and educational institutions that offered ES/CS training programs to their employees: California State University, New York Dept. Of Labor, United Way of Maryland, Affinity Health Plan, Harvard Pilgrim Health Care, U.S. General Accounting Office (GAO), Harvard University, U.S. Postal Service, CNN/Turner Broadcasting, Jack Henry & Associates, John Hancock Insurance Co., Verizon, Prudential Insurance, Bank of America, Massachusetts Institute of Technology, Brigham and Women's Hospital, Mt. Sinai Medical Center, and others.

NOTES

LESSON 1: Simple Words

Definition of Simple Words

A Simple Word is a word without a prefix or suffix. EasyScript uses two techniques for short simple words and for long simple words.

One and Two Letter Abbreviations

For shorter words, use a *one* and *two-letter* code made up of letters which are part of a word or leave out all or some of the vowels.

If a given word can be abbreviated in more than one way, easy memorization and fast transcription should be your determining factors.

To expand your abbreviating choices you can use the phonic technique which uses sounds associated with the word, for example, z = as, k = can.

Three Letter Abbreviations

For longer words, use two following options:

First 3: Use the first 3 letters of the word as your abbreviation.

Two + 1: Use the first 2 letters and the last letter of the word as your abbreviation.

We recommend to use **First 3** as your *main option* and **Two + 1** as an *alternative* for certain words ONLY.

For example, for the words *analyze, analysis and analyst*, the **First 3** rule will produce the same code for all these words. In this case, you can continue to use the **First 3** rule and rely completely on context to interpret, or you can use the **Two + 1** rule which produces a different code for each word as an alternative.

Studying Alphabetical Abbreviations

Write and memorize the alphabetical abbreviations in the space provided.

One-letter codes

and (**d**) _____	in (**n**) _____	the (**h**) _____
as (**z**) _____	is (**s**) _____	to (**t**) _____
be (**b**) _____	may (**m**) _____	you (**u**) _____
very (**v**) _____	good (**g**) _____	see (**c**) _____
of (**o**) _____	we (**w**) _____	if (**f**) _____

NOTES

Two-letter codes

any (**ny**) _____   have (**hv**) _____

was (**ws**) _____   are (**ar**) _____

like (**lk**) _____   week (**wk**) _____

due (**du**) _____   new (**nw**) _____

were (**wr**) _____   for (**fr**) _____

our (**ou**) _____   will (**wl**) _____

from (**fm**) _____   than (**tn**) _____

would (**wd**)_____   has (**hs**) _____

that (**th**) _____   your (**yr**) _____

Phrases

the following (**tf**) _____

thank you (**ty**) _____

Very truly yours (**vty**) _____

Long Words

Write alphabetical abbreviations for the following words using the approach described earlier:

	First 3	2 + 1
merchandise (**mer**)	_____	
curriculum (**cur**)	_____	
knowledge (**kno**)	_____	

NOTES

	First 3		2 + 1
analyze (**ana**) _____		(**ane**) _____	
analysis (**ana**) _____		(**ans**) _____	
analyst (**ana**) _____		(**ant**) _____	

We recommend using **First 3** as a main option and **Two + 1** as an alternative for the words that have multiple meanings for the same code.

Practicing Alphabetical Abbreviations

Write the appropriate alphabetical abbreviations memorized from the previous exercise.

One-letter codes

and _____	in _____	the _____
as _____	is _____	to _____
be _____	may _____	you _____
very _____	good _____	see _____
of _____	we _____	if _____

Two-letter codes

any _____	have _____
was _____	are _____
like _____	week _____
due _____	new _____
were _____	for _____
our _____	will _____

NOTES

from _____   than _____

would_____   has _____

that _____   your _____

Phrases

the following   _____

thank you   _____

Very truly yours   _____

Long Words

Write alphabetical abbreviations for the following words using the approach described on page 3.

	First 3	2 + 1
merchandise	_____	
curriculum	_____	
knowledge	_____	
analyze	_____	_____
analysis	_____	_____
analyst	_____	_____

Read and study examples below:

Many people will partake in this event.
Mn pp wl par (pae) n ts ev.

Merchandise was not sent on time.
Mer (mee) ws nt sn on tm.

NOTES

Studying Symbol Forms

Study and memorize the symbols to write each letter of the alphabet:

MINISCRIPT SYMBOLS		
A ˙	B ˙	C .
D ʼ	E ʼ	F ʼ
G ʻ	H ʻ	I ʻ
J >	K >	L >
M <	N <	O <
P)	Q)	R)
S ⁻	T –	U _
V ^	W ^	X ^
Y (	Z (	

NOTES

Study and memorize alphabetical abbreviations and symbol forms for the words below.

One-symbol forms

	Alphabetical abbreviation	Symbol form
and	d	,
in	n	<
the	h	'
as	z	(
is	s	—
to	t	—
be	b	•
may	m	<
you	u	—
very	v	^
of	o	<
we	w	^
if	f	,

Two-symbol forms

	Alphabetical abbreviation	Symbol form
any	ny	(<
have	hv	^ '

8

NOTES

Word	Alphabetical abbreviation	Symbol form
was	ws	
are	ar	
like	lk	
week	wk	
due	du	
new	nw	
were	wr	
for	fr	
our	ou	
will	wl	
from	fm	
than	tn	
would	wd	
has	hs	
that	th	
your	yr	

Three-symbol forms

	Alphabetical abbreviation	Symbol form
able	abl	
fill	fll	

NOTES

should	shd	
about	abt	
find	fnd	
then	thn	
also	als	
firm	frm	

Phrases

	Alphabetical abbreviation	Symbol form
the following	tf	
thank you	ty	
Very truly yours	vty	

Study and memorize symbol forms for the words using the First 3 and Two + 1 rules:

	First 3	2 + 1
particular (**par**)		
merchandise (**mer**)		
curriculum (**cur**)		
knowledge (**kno**)		
analyze (**ana ane**)		
analysis (**ana ans**)		
analyst (**ana ant**)		

NOTES

Practicing Symbol Forms

Write the appropriate symbol forms memorized from the previous exercise:

and _____

in _____

the _____

as _____

is _____

to _____

be _____

may _____

you _____

very _____

of _____

we _____

if _____

any _____

have _____

was _____

are _____

like _____

week _____

NOTES

due _____

new _____

were _____

for _____

our _____

will _____

from _____

than _____

would _____

has _____

that _____

your _____

able _____

fill _____

should _____

about _____

find _____

then _____

also _____

firm _____

NOTES

Phrases

the following	**tf**	
thank you	**ty**	
Very truly yours	**vty**	

Write symbol forms for the following words using the First 3 and Two + 1 rules:

		First 3	**2 + 1**
particular	_____		
merchandise	_____		
curriculum	_____		
knowledge	_____		
analyze	_____		
analysis	_____		
analyst	_____		

Days

Sunday	**su**	
Monday	**mo**	
Tuesday	**tu**	
Wednesday	**wn**	
Thursday	**th**	
Friday	**fr**	
Saturday	**sa**	

NOTES

Months

January	**jan**	
February	**feb**	
March	**mar**	
April	**apr**	
May	**may**	
June	**jun**	
July	**jul**	
August	**aug**	
September	**sep**	
October	**oct**	
November	**nov**	
December	**dec**	

* A date can be also abbreviated as: May 1 = 5/1.

NOTES

LESSON 2: Prefix Words

Definition of Prefix Words

Any word which has a root with a prefix participle placed before it is a prefix word. The list of frequently used prefixes is given below and they are abbreviated with one letter as shown in the parenthesis.

Studying EasyScript Abbreviations

Prefix rule

To abbreviate a prefix word use the prefix symbol + SCR (Straight Count Root) or OVR (Omit Vowel Root).

Example:

```
                s                1 2
SUBDIVIDE >   SUB      -      D I V I D E
              \ | /           \ \ | / /
             Prefix            Root
```
The resulting abbreviations are:

sdi	**sdv**
SCR	OVR

Writing the Root

You can have two options writing roots: Straight Count Root (SCR) or Omit Vowel Root (OVR).

1) Both SCR and OVR roots are written with 2 letters.

2) SCR starts always with the FIRST root letter.

3) OVR is a form of abbreviation where you omit all or some of the vowels in the root. This option is available for users who prefer writing without the vowels. The following guidelines will help you to gain better understanding of this concept:

— before writing an actual abbreviation each prefix word MUST BE BROKEN down into a prefix and a root

— although a prefix and a root are a part of the same abbreviation they are abbreviated SEPARATELY

— the count of 2 letters DOES NOT include the prefix symbol. When you use the SCR option, always abbreviate the root starting with the FIRST root letter

— when you use the OVR option, omit the ROOT vowels only. You should never apply omitting the vowels for abbreviating the prefixes.

NOTES

This list of prefixes has been carefully thought out and serves most people well. However, if you find that using one of these symbols slows you down, choose one that facilitates your writing. For example: you can use N for "en" as opposed to "e" which is shown on the list.

Write and memorize prefix letters in the space provided:

ac, ap, as (**a**) _____   com, con (**c**) _____

de, dis (**d**) _____   en (**e**) _____

ex (**x**) _____   for, fore (**f**) _____

in, im, inter (**i**) _____

pro, pre, per (**p**) _____

re, ir (**r**) _____

sub, sup, super (**s**) _____

tran, trans (**t**) _____

un, under (**u**) _____

Write alphabetical abbreviations in each column for the words below using the prefix rule:

Example:

	SCR	OVR
p 12 pro - l o n g	plo	pln
x 12 ex - p e c t	_____	_____
i 12 in - f o r m	_____	_____
r 12 re - q u e s t	_____	_____

NOTES

f   1 2
<u>for</u> - w a r d   _____   _____

c   1 2
<u>con</u> - t e s t   _____   _____

d   1 2
<u>dis</u> - c o u n t   _____   _____

e   1 2
<u>en</u> - c l o s e   _____   _____

a   1 2
<u>ap</u> - p r a i s e   _____   _____

t   1 2
<u>tran</u> - s c r i b e   _____   _____

s   1 2
<u>sub</u> - d i v i d e   _____   _____

r   1 2
<u>re</u> - c o m m e n d   _____   _____

i   1 2
<u>im</u> - p o s s i b l e   _____   _____

Rd d tcr tf :

Ths sy wl icl tf ks : rtr, dl, rpl, ctr, rtu (rtn) n d ise (ist). F h usr types ps h mar h tx wl cti (ctn) on tf ln. Pl fwa (fwd) h eti (etr) am n 5 ds fm h rce (rct) o ths letter. F u do nt rsp h owr wl ist us t bg h pce (pcs) t evi (evc) u.

NOTES

Practicing EasyScript Abbreviations

Write and memorize prefix letters in the space provided:

ac, ap, as   _____   com, con _____

de, dis   _____   en   _____

ex   _____   for, fore   _____

in, im, inter   _____   _____

pro, pre, per   _____   _____

re, ir   _____   _____

sub, sup, super   _____   _____

tran, trans   _____   _____

un, under   _____   _____

Write alphabetical abbreviations for the words below using the prefix rule:

	SCR	OVR
com - pass	_____	_____
con - test	_____	_____
per - sonnel	_____	_____
pre - arrange	_____	_____
pro - duct	_____	_____
ex - pand	_____	_____
ex - cuse	_____	_____
im - pose	_____	_____

NOTES

in - put   _____   _____

inter - rupt   _____   _____

re - peat   _____   _____

re - turn   _____   _____

de - termine   _____   _____

de - lay   _____   _____

dis - play   _____   _____

ac - credit   _____   _____

ap - praise   _____   _____

as - sure   _____   _____

en - close   _____   _____

for - ward   _____   _____

fore - cast   _____   _____

sub - divide   _____   _____

sup - pose   _____   _____

trans - port   _____   _____

tran - sit   _____   _____

un - certain   _____   _____

under - stand   _____   _____

NOTES

Studying MiniScript Forms

Study and memorize alphabetical abbreviations and symbol forms:

MINISCRIPT SYMBOLS		
A ·	**B** ·	**C** .
D '	**E** '	**F** '
G '	**H** '	**I** '
J >	**K** >	**L** >
M <	**N** <	**O** <
P)	**Q**)	**R**)
S ⁻	**T** ⁻	**U** ⁻
V ^	**W** ^	**X** ^
Y (	**Z** (	

NOTES

ac, ap, as	**a**		com, con	**c**
de, dis	**d**		en	**e**
ex	**x**		for, fore	**f**
in, im, inter	**i**			
pro, pre, per	**p**			
re, ir	**r**			
sub, sup, super	**s**			
tran, trans	**t**			
un, under	**u**			

	SCR	OVR	SCR	OVR
p 12 pro - l o n g	plo	pln		
x 12 ex - p e c t	xpe	xpt		
i 12 in - f o r m	ifo	ifm		
r 12 re - q u e s t	rqu	rqt		
f 1 2 for - w a r d	fwa	fwd		
c 12 con - t e s t	cte	ctt		
d 12 dis - c o u n t	dco	dct		

NOTES

e 12				
en - c l o s e	ecl	ecs		

a 12				
ap - p r a i s e	apr	aps		

t 12				
tran - s c r i b e	tsc	tsb		

s 12				
sub - d i v i d e	sdi	sdv		

r 12				
re - c o m m e n d	rco	rcm		

i 1234				
im - p o s s i b l e	ipo	ipb		

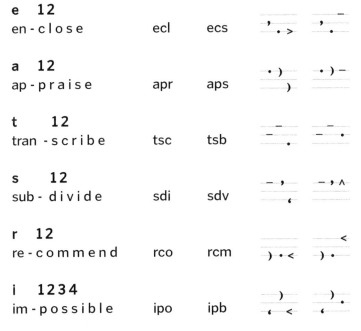

Rd d tcr tf: (when applicable both **SCR** and **OVR** shown):

Ths sy wl icl tf ks: rtr, dl, rpl, ctr, rtu (rtn) n d ise (ist). F h usr types ps h mar h tx wl cti (ctn) on tf ln. Pl fwa (fwd) h eti (etr) am n 5 ds fm h rce (rct) o ths letter. F u do nt rsp h owr wl ist us t bg h pce (pcs) t evi (evc) u.

Write corresponding symbol forms for the text above.

Please note abbreviations for some words above with OVR option are written by using the first and last letter. However, if using cts for contest is easier for you than ctt you should choose the option that makes you writing faster.

NOTES

Practicing EasyScript Abbreviations and MiniScript Forms

Write symbol forms for the prefixes below:

ac, ap, as	a _____	com, con	c _____
de, dis	d _____	en	e _____
ex	x _____	for, fore	f _____
in, im, inter	i _____		
pro, pre, per	p _____		
re, ir	r _____		
sub, sup, super	s _____		
tran, trans	t _____		
un, under	u _____		

Write symbol forms for the words below:

	SCR	OVR
p 12 pro - l o n g	_____	_____
x 12 ex - p e c t	_____	_____
i 12 in - f o r m	_____	_____
r 12 re - q u e s t	_____	_____
f 12 for - w a r d	_____	_____

NOTES

c 12
con - t e s t

d 12
dis - c o u n t

e 12
en - c l o s e

a 12
ap - p r a i s e

t 12
tran - s c r i b e

s 12
sub - d i v i d e

r 12
re - c o m m e n d

i 1234
im - p o s s i b l e

Write the alphabetical abbreviations and symbol forms for the following:

ac ap as	_____	con com	_____
de dis	_____	for fore	_____
im in inter	_____	en	_____
pro pre per	_____	re ir	_____
ex	_____	un under	_____
sub sup super	_____	tran trans	_____

NOTES

Write alphabetical abbreviations and symbol forms for the words below:

	Alphabetical abbreviation	Symbol form
com - pass	_____	
con - test	_____	
per - sonnel	_____	
pre - arrange	_____	
pro - duct	_____	
ex - pand	_____	
ex - cuse	_____	
im - pose	_____	
in - put	_____	
inter - rupt	_____	
re - peat	_____	
re - turn	_____	
de - termine	_____	
de - lay	_____	
dis - play	_____	
ac - credit	_____	
ap - praise	_____	
as - sure	_____	

NOTES

en - close _____ ─────────

for - ward _____ ─────────

fore - cast _____ ─────────

sub - divide _____ ─────────

sup - pose _____ ─────────

trans - port _____ ─────────

tran - sit _____ ─────────

un - certain _____ ─────────

under - stand _____ ─────────

Practicing MiniScript Forms

Write alphabetical abbreviations and symbol forms for the words below:

	SCR		OVR	
com - pass	_____	─────	_____	─────
con - test	_____	─────	_____	─────
per - sonnel	_____	─────	_____	─────
pre - arrange*	_____	─────	_____	─────
pro - duct	_____	─────	_____	─────
ex - pand	_____	─────	_____	─────
ex - cuse	_____	─────	_____	─────

* When a word is marked with * both SCR and OVR are identical.

NOTES

im - pose _____

in - put _____

inter - rupt _____

re - peat _____

re - turn _____

de - termine _____

de - lay _____

dis - play _____

ac - credit* _____

ap - praise* _____

as - sure _____

en - close* _____

for - ward _____

fore - cast _____

sub - divide _____

sup - pose _____

trans - port _____

tran - sit _____

un - certain _____

under - stand* _____

NOTES

LESSON 3: Suffix Words

Definition of Suffix Words

Any word which has a root with a suffix participle placed after it is a suffix word. The list of frequently used suffixes is given below. They are abbreviated with one letter as shown in the parentheses.

Studying EasyScript Abbreviations

Suffix rule

To abbreviate suffix words use the SCR root or OVR root + the suffix symbol

Example:

```
          1 2
SUCCESSFUL >  S U C C E S S  - FUL
              \ | /       \ | /
              ROOT       SUFFIX
```

The resulting abbreviations are:

SCR	OVR
suf	scf

Writing the Root

You can have two options to use: Straight Count Root (SCR) or Omit Vowel Root (OVR)

1) the root, either SCR or OVR, is written with 2 letters.
2) Straight Count Root (the column designated as SCR) starts always with the FIRST root letter.

The SCR roots start always with the FIRST ROOT LETTER.

1) the root is written with 2 letters (the column designated as SCR)
2) Omit Vowel Root (the column designated as OVR). This option is available for users who prefer to write without the vowels. The following guidelines will help you to gain a better understanding of this concept:
— before writing an actual abbreviation each suffix word MUST BE BROKEN down into a suffix and a root
— although a suffix and a root are a part of the same abbreviation they are abbreviated SEPARATELY

NOTES

— the count of 2 letters DOES NOT include the suffix symbol. When you use the SCR option, always abbreviate the root starting with the FIRST root letter

— when you use the OVR option, omit the ROOT vowels only. You should never omit the vowels for abbreviating the suffixes

— when you use the OVR option, do not omit the vowel in the first root position. For example, if you abbreviate the word "administrator" using the OVR option and omit the vowel "a," it will make transcription more difficult.

This list of prefixes has been carefully thought out and serves most people well. However if you find that using one of these symbols slows you down, choose one that facilitates your writing. For example, you can use R for "ure" as opposed to "u" which is shown on the list.

Write and memorize suffix letters in the space provided:

ABLE, IBLE **(b)** _____   AGE, ING **(g)** _____

AL **(l)** _____   ANCE, ENCE **(c)** _____

ANT, ENT, NESS **(n)** _____

ATE, EST, IST **(t)** _____

ES, OUS, LESS **(s)** _____

ER, OR **(r)** _____   FUL **(f)** _____

IC **(k)** _____   ISM, MENT **(m)** _____

IVE **(v)** _____   IZE **(z)** _____

SHIP **(p)** _____   SION, TION **(h)** _____

URE **(u)** _____

Write alphabetical abbreviations in each column for the words below using the suffix rule:

	SCR	OVR
12 r		
f a c t - or	_____	_____

NOTES

1 2   g
m e e t - ing   _____ _____

12   u
p l e a s - ure   _____ _____

12   l
c l a s s i c - al   _____ _____

12   d
c r e d i t - ed   _____ _____

12   k
d r a m a t - ic   _____ _____

12   d
s p e c i f i - ed   _____ _____

12 s
p r i c - es   _____ _____

12 s
l i s t - less   _____ _____

1 2   s
n u m e r - ous   _____ _____

12 c
a l l i - ance   _____ _____

12 c
e v i d - ence   _____ _____

12 b
a v a i l - able   _____ _____

12   n
d i f f e r - ent   _____ _____

12   n
q u i c k - ness   _____ _____

30

NOTES

12   **y**
<u>o c c u p a n</u> - cy   _____   _____

12   **y**
<u>v o l u n t a</u> - ry   _____   _____

12   **y**
<u>s t a b i l i</u> - ty   _____   _____

12   **h**
<u>a t t e n</u> - tion   _____   _____

12   **h**
<u>d i m e n</u> - sion   _____   _____

12   **t**
<u>e a r l i</u> - est   _____   _____

12   **t**
<u>h e s i t</u> - ate   _____   _____

12   **t**
<u>s c i e n</u> - ist   _____   _____

12   **v**
<u>t e n t a t</u> - ive   _____   _____

12   **m**
<u>s h i p</u> - ment   _____   _____

12   **p**
<u>s p a c e</u> - ship   _____   _____

Tcr tf: (when applicable both SCR and OVR shown):

1. W hv md a din (dfn) arm n ou rn coh (clh). H ler (ltr) sps th h pam pey (pny) wd b at h oph o h bn.

2. W smi (smt) tf lst o ses (svs) avb fr yr spl fig (flg). Atc at h spl pmi (pmt) heg (hrg) d ny chs n drgs wl b dn on an hry bs. Ady, ths tm fm s sje (sjt) t obg dt fm yr pje (pjt) adr r cor (crd). Cur (csr) mac (mnc) cn b dn at an afb rt.

NOTES

1. _____

_____

_____

_____

2. _____

_____

_____

_____

_____

_____

_____

Practicing EasyScript Abbreviations

Write and memorize suffix letters in the space provided:

ABLE, IBLE	_____	AGE, ING	_____
AL	_____	ANCE, ENCE	_____
ANT, ENT, NESS	_____		
ATE, EST, IST	_____		
ES, OUS, LESS	_____		
ER, OR	_____	FUL	_____
IC	_____	ISM, MENT	_____
IVE	_____	IZE	_____
SHIP	_____	SION, TION	_____
URE	_____		

NOTES

Write alphabetical abbreviations for the words below using the suffix rule:

	SCR	OVR
addition - al	_____	_____
sever - al	_____	_____
credit - ed	_____	_____
suggest -ed	_____	_____
bas - ed	_____	_____
advantag - es	_____	_____
pric - es	_____	_____
sampl - es	_____	_____
bottom - less	_____	_____
numer - ous	_____	_____
administrat - or	_____	_____
answ - er	_____	_____
manufactur - er	_____	_____
off - er	_____	_____
attend - ance	_____	_____
occurr - ence	_____	_____
espion - age	_____	_____
obtain - ing	_____	_____
afford - able	_____	_____

NOTES

brilli - ant   _____   _____

differ - ent   _____   _____

bitter - ness   _____   _____

efficien - cy   _____   _____

satisfacto - ry   _____   _____

opportuni - ty   _____   _____

additional - ly   _____   _____

ear - ly   _____   _____

kind - ly   _____   _____

month - ly   _____   _____

mat - ure   _____   _____

documenta - tion   _____   _____

dimen - sion   _____   _____

smart - est   _____   _____

earli - est   _____   _____

fast - est   _____   _____

separ - ate   _____   _____

psychiatr - ist   _____   _____

administrat - ive   _____   _____

arrange - ment   _____   _____

equip - ment   _____   _____

NOTES

ship - ment   _____   _____

state - ment   _____   _____

success - ful   _____   _____

characterist - ic   _____   _____

member - ship   _____   _____

Studying MiniScript Forms

MINISCRIPT SYMBOLS		
A ·	B ·	C ·
D '	E '	F '
G '	H '	I '
J >	K >	L >
M <	N <	O <
P)	Q)	R)
S ‾	T ‾	U ‾
V ^	W ^	X ^
Y (	Z (	

NOTES

Study and memorize suffix alphabetical abbreviations and symbol forms below:

ABLE, IBLE	b	·	AGE, ING	g	‘
AL	l	>	ANCE, ENCE	c	·
ANT, ENT, NESS	n	<			
ATE, EST, IST	t	—			
ES, OUS, LESS	s	—			
ER, OR	r	)	FUL	f	,
IC	k	>	ISM, MENT	m	<
IVE	v	^	IZE	z	(
SHIP	p	)	SION, TION	h	‘
URE	u	—			

		SCR	OVR		SCR	OVR
12	**r**					
f a c t – or		far	fcr		· ,)	, ·)
12	**g**					
m e e t - ing		meg	mtg		< ‘ ,	< ‘ —
12	**u**					
p l e a s - ure		plu	plu		) > —	) > —
12	**l**					
c l a s sic - al		cll	cll		· > >	· > >
12	**d**					
c r e d it - ed		crd	crd		, ·)	, ·)
12	**k**					
d r a m at - ic		drk	drk		, >)	, >)

NOTES

12	**d**			
s p e c i f i - ed	spd	spd		

12	**s**			
p r i c - es	prs	prs		

12	**s**			
l i s t - less	lis	lis		

12	**s**			
n u m e r - ous	nus	nms		

12	**c**			
a l l i - ance	alc	alc		

12	**c**			
e v i d - ence	evc	evc		

12	**b**			
a v a i l - able	avb	avb		

12	**n**			
d i f f e r - ent	din	dfn		

12	**n**			
q u i c k - ness	qun	qkn		

12	**y**			
o c c u p a n - cy	ocy	ocy		

12	**y**			
v o l u n t a - ry	voy	vly		

12	**y**			
s t a b i l i - ty	sty	sty		

12	**h**			
a t t e n - tion	ath	ath		

12	**h**			
d i m e n - sion	dih	dmh		

NOTES

12	t			
e a r l i - est	eat	ert		

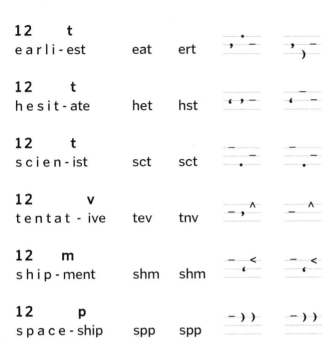

12	t			
h e s i t - ate	het	hst		

12	t			
s c i e n - ist	sct	sct		

12	v			
t e n t a t - ive	tev	tnv		

12	m			
s h i p - ment	shm	shm		

12	p			
s p a c e - ship	spp	spp		

Rd d tcr tf: (when applicable both SCR and OVR shown):

W hv mde a din (dfn) arm n ou rnt coh (clh). H ler (ltr) sps th h pam pey (pny) wd b at h oph o h bnk. Pls lt us knw h dt on whh u wl rse (rsv) h ney (ncy) eqm.

W smi (smt) tf lst o ses (svs) avb fr yr spl fig (flg). Atc at h Spl Pmi (Pmt) Heg (Hrg) d ny chs n drgs wl b dn on an hry bs. Ady, ths tm fm s sje (sjc) t obg dt fm yr Pje (Pjc) Adr r Cor. Cur (Csr) mac (mnc) cn b dn at an afb rt.

Write corresponding symbols forms for the texts above:

NOTES

Practicing EasyScript Abbreviations and MiniScript Forms

Write symbol forms for the suffixes below:

ABLE, IBLE	b		AGE, ING	g	
AL	l		ANCE, ENCE	c	
ANT, ENT, NESS	n				
ATE, EST, IST	t				
ES, OUS, LESS	s				
ER, OR	r		FUL	f	
IC	k		ISM, MENT	m	
IVE	v		IZE	z	
SHIP	p		SION, TION	h	
URE	u				

Write symbol forms for the words below:

		SCR	OVR
12	**r**		
f a c t – or			
12	**g**		
m e e t - ing			
12	**u**		
p l e a s - ure			
12	**l**		
c l a s sic - al			

NOTES

12   d
c r e d i t - ed

12   k
d r a m a t - ic

12   d
s p e c i f i - ed

12   s
p r i c - es

12   s
l i s t - less

12   s
n u m e r - ous

12   c
a l l i - ance

12   c
e v i d - ence

12   b
a v a i l - able

12   n
d i f f e r - ent

12   n
q u i c k - ness

12   y
o c c u pan - cy

12   y
v o l u n t a - ry

12   y
s t a b i l i - ty

NOTES

12   **h**
a t t e n - tion

12   **h**
d i m e n - sion

12   **t**
e a r l i - est

12   **t**
h e s i t - ate

12   **t**
s c i e n - ist

12   **v**
t e n t a t - ive

12   **m**
s h i p - ment

12   **p**
s p a c e - ship

Write the alphabetical abbreviations and symbol forms for the following:

ABLE, IBLE   _____   AGE, ING   _____

AL   _____   ANCE, ENCE   _____

ANT, ENT, NESS   _____

ATE, EST, IST   _____

ES, OUS, LESS   _____

ER, OR   _____   FUL   _____

IC   _____   ISM, MENT   _____

NOTES

IVE	_____	IZE	_____
SHIP	_____	SION, TION	_____
URE	_____		

Write the alphabetical abbreviations and symbol forms for the words below:

	Alphabetical abbreviation	Symbol form
addition - al	_____	
sever - al	_____	
credit - ed	_____	
suggest -ed	_____	
bas - ed	_____	
advantag - es	_____	
pric - es	_____	
sampl - es	_____	
bottom - less	_____	
numer - ous	_____	
administrat - or	_____	
answ - er	_____	
manufactur - er	_____	
off - er	_____	
attend - ance	_____	

42

NOTES

occurr - ence   _____

espion - age   _____

obtain - ing   _____

afford - able   _____

brilli - ant   _____

differ - ent   _____

bitter - ness   _____

efficien - cy   _____

satisfacto - ry   _____

opportuni - ty   _____

additional - ly   _____

ear - ly   _____

kind - ly   _____

month - ly   _____

mat - ure   _____

documenta - tion _____

dimen - sion   _____

smart - est   _____

earli - est   _____

fast - est   _____

NOTES

separ - ate _____

psychiatr - ist _____

administrat - ive _____

arrange - ment _____

equip - ment _____

ship - ment _____

state - ment _____

success - ful _____

characterist - ic _____

member - ship _____

Practicing MiniScript Forms

Write alphabetical abbreviations and symbol forms for the words below:

	SCR	OVR
addition - al*	_____	_____
sever - al	_____	_____
credit - ed*	_____	_____
suggest -ed	_____	_____
bas - ed	_____	_____
advantag - es*	_____	_____

* When a word is marked with * both SCR and OVR are identical.

NOTES

pric - es*   _____   _____

sampl - es   _____   _____

bottom - less   _____   _____

numer - ous   _____   _____

administrat - or*   _____   _____

answ - er*   _____   _____

manufactur - er   _____   _____

off - er*   _____   _____

attend - ance*   _____   _____

occurr - ence*   _____   _____

espion - age*   _____   _____

obtain - ing*   _____   _____

afford - able*   _____   _____

brilli - ant*   _____   _____

differ - ent   _____   _____

bitter - ness   _____   _____

efficien - cy*   _____   _____

satisfacto - ry   _____   _____

opportuni - ty*   _____   _____

additional - ly*   _____   _____

NOTES

ear - ly _____ _____ _____ _____

kind - ly _____ _____ _____ _____

month - ly _____ _____ _____ _____

mat - ure _____ _____ _____ _____

documenta - tion _____ _____ _____ _____

dimen - sion _____ _____ _____ _____

smart - est* _____ _____ _____ _____

earli - est _____ _____ _____ _____

fast - est _____ _____ _____ _____

separ - ate _____ _____ _____ _____

psychiatr - ist* _____ _____ _____ _____

administrat - ive* _____ _____ _____ _____

arrange - ment* _____ _____ _____ _____

equip - ment* _____ _____ _____ _____

ship - ment* _____ _____ _____ _____

state - ment* _____ _____ _____ _____

success - ful _____ _____ _____ _____

characterist - ic* _____ _____ _____ _____

member - ship _____ _____ _____ _____

NOTES

LESSON 4: Prefix/Suffix Words

Definition of Prefix/Suffix Words

Any word which has a root with a prefix and a suffix participle placed after it is a prefix/suffix word.

Studying Alphabetical Abbreviations and Symbol Forms

Prefix/Suffix Rule

To abbreviate Prefix/Suffix words use the prefix symbol + one root letter + the suffix symbol.

EXAMPLE: COMPARTMENT >

```
c          1      m
COM -   P A R T  - MENT
 \|/       \|/      \|/
```

PREFIX   ROOT   SUFFIX

The resulting abbreviation is: **CPM**

Write the alphabetical abbreviations:

```
r   1        m
re – q u i r e - ment          _____
```

```
x   1            h
con – s i d e r a - tion        _____
```

```
r   1      g
re – v i e w - ing             _____
```

```
u   1                y
un – s a t i s f a c to - ry     _____
```

47

NOTES

PREFIXES

Study and memorize the alphabetical abbreviations and symbol forms below:

AC, AP, AS	a		COM, CON	c	
DE, DIS	d		EN	e	
EX	x		FOR, FORE	f	
IN, IM, INTER	i				
PRO, PRE, PER	p				
RE, IR	r				
SUB, SUP, SUPER	s				
TRAN, TRANS	t				
UN, UNDER	u				

SUFFIXES

ABLE, IBLE	b		AGE, ING	g	
AL	l		ANCE, ENCE	c	
ANT, ENT, NESS	n				
ATE, EST, IST	t				
ES, OUS, LESS	s				
ER, OR	r		FUL	f	
IC	k		ISM, MENT	m	
IVE	v		IZE	z	
SHIP	p		SION, TION	h	
URE	u				

48

NOTES

r 1 m			
re – q u i r e - ment	rqm		

x 1 h			
con – s i d e r a - tion	csh		

r 1 g			
re – v i e w - ing	rvg		

u 1 y			
un – s a t i s f a c to - ry	usy		

Practicing Alphabetical Abbreviations and Symbol Forms

Write the alphabetical abbreviations and symbol forms for the following:

	ES	MS*		ES	MS
PREFIXES					
ac ap	_____		con com	_____	
de dis	_____		for fore	_____	
im in inter	_____		en	_____	
pro pre per	_____		re ir	_____	
ex	_____		un under	_____	
sub sup super	_____		tran trans	_____	
SUFFIXES					
able, ible	_____		age, ing	_____	
al	_____		ance, ence	_____	
ant, ent, ness	_____		ate, est, ist	_____	

* MS = MiniScript

NOTES

es, ous, less   _____

er, or   _____   ful   _____

ic   _____   ism, ment   _____

ive   _____   ize   _____

ship   _____   sion, tion   _____

ure   _____

Write the symbol forms for the following:

PREFIXES

ac ap		com con	
de dis		for fore	
im in inter		en	
pro pre per		re ir	
ex		un under	
sub sup super		tran trans	

SUFFIXES

able ible		age ing	
al ance ence			
ant ent ness		ate est ist	
cy ly ty ry		ed	
er or		es ous less	
ful		ic	
ism ment		ive	

NOTES

ize		ship	
sion tion		ure	

Write the alphabetical abbreviations and symbol forms for the words below:

	Alphabetical abbreviation	**Symbol form**
con-verse-ly	_____	
con-sistent-ly	_____	
consideration	_____	
re-sponsibili-ty	_____	
re-lev-ant	_____	
re-ceiv-ed	_____	
re-view-ing	_____	
re-quest-ed	_____	
investigate	_____	
in-telligent-ly	_____	
en-tire-ly	_____	
investment	_____	
im-port-ance	_____	
in-sur-ed	_____	
en-clos-ed	_____	
con-troll-ed	_____	
con-troll-ing	_____	
con-cern-ing	_____	

NOTES

un-avoid-able _____

com-fort-able _____

com-p-ly _____

requirement _____

re-presentat-ive _____

re-p-ly _____

de-mand-ing _____

un-satisfacto-ry _____

de-let-ed _____

pro-perti-es _____

pro-motion-al _____

in-depend-ent _____

com-municat-ed _____

com-petit-ive _____

im-port-ant _____

im-prove-ment _____

ex-haust-ed _____

in-decis-ive _____

in-struc-tion _____

con-veni-ence _____

sup-p-ly _____

NOTES

Practicing MiniScript Forms

Write the symbol forms for the following words:

con - verse - ly

con - sistent - ly

com - p – ly

con - sidera – tion

re - sponsibili - ty

re - lev – ant

re - p – ly

re - view - ing

re - quest - ed

in - vestig – ate

in - telligent - ly

sup - p – ly

in - vest - ment

im - port - ance

in - sur - ed

con - troll - ed

con - troll - ing

con - cern - ing

com - fort - able

re - quire - ment

NOTES

re - ceiv - ed

re - presentat - ive

de - mand - ing

de - let - ed

pro - perti - es

pro - motion - al

in - depend - ent

com - municat - ed

com - petit - ive

im - port - ant

im - prove - ment

in - decis - ive

in - struc – tion

con - veni - ence

in - troduc - ing

im - prov - ed

com - munica - tion

pro - cess - ing

pro - gress - ed

pro - ductivi – ty

un - success - ful

un - satisfacto - ry

NOTES

de - velop - er

in - dic - ate

com - puter - ize

un - resolv - ed

un - avoid - able

ac - cord - ance

ac - knowledg - ed

ap - preciat - ed

en - clos - ing

en - clos - ed

en - tire - ly

ex - haust - ed

1. Cvery, mst csisy sucf limd parrs acep rspoy t ivest potl genl parrs. 1 o h elems t csidr whn rvieg h stru o a limd parp s potl cfli o itert. Addy, a limd parr shl b pvid wth h rlevn info durg h lst sevl oprg qrtrs.

2. Sucf limd parrs ctin t wrk z itely at thr ivesms z thy did t mke thir mny n h 1st plce. T elat on ou csidh o h genl parrs iporc t yr ivesm succ, w wl nw lk int sme o h crtl aras ctrod by genl parrs. H limd parrs n trn ows it t h/slf t rvie al doch d corc cary d t rais quehs ccerg cfli abt whh he do' fel cforb.

Write the corresponding symbol forms for the texts above.

1. _____

2. _____

NOTES

LESSON 5: Compound Words

Definition of compound words

Any word which is composed of two or more words is a compound word.

Compound Rules

Studying Alphabetical Abbreviations

Read the rules and write the appropriate abbreviations using each rule.

Simple compound

Use the first letter of the first word followed by a slash sign (\) or (/) and up to 2 first or up to 2 non-vowel letters of the second word. The choice between (\) or (/) is available for right-handed and left-handed users.

Example:

	SC	OV
AIR / CRAFT	a\cr a\cra	a\crt

Write the appropriate abbreviations for the words below:

	SC	OV
club/house		
copy/right		
blood/test		

Suffix Compound

Use the first letter of the first word followed by a slash sign (\) or (/) and 2 first or 2 non-vowel letters of the second word + the suffix symbol.

Example:

	SC	OV
GUIDE /LIN - ES	g/is	g/ns

NOTES

Write the appropriate abbreviations for the words below:

	SC	OV
peace/maker		
photo/copying		
how/ever		
counter/offer		
counter/measure		

To avoid transcription problems when you utilize the non-vowel option, do not omit the vowel in the first position.

Prefix Compound

Use the first letter of the first word followed by a slash sign(\) or (/) and prefix symbol + 2 next or 2 non-vowel letters of the second word.

Example:

	SC	OV
OVER / EX - POSE	o/xpo	o/xps

Write the appropriate abbreviations for the words below:

	SC	OV
over/protect		
over/extend		

Prefix/Suffix Compound

Use the first letter of the first word followed by a slash sign (\) or (/) and prefix symbol, 1 root letter and suffix symbol of the second word.

Example:

COUNTER / PRO - POS - AL   c/pl

NOTES

Write the appropriate abbreviations for the words below:

over/development

over/production

counter/productive

Practicing Alphabetical Abbreviations

Write the appropriate abbreviations for the words below (SC - Straight Count, OV - Omit Vowels):

Simple Compound

Example: buzzword > buzz / word - b/wo b/wd

	SC	OV
bath/room		
court/yard		
chair/man		
girl/friend		
electro/therapy		
boy/friend		
main/stream		
down/turn		
down/hill		
bench/mark		
class/room		
water/front		
flash/light		
there/fore		

NOTES

Prefix Compound

Example: overproduce > over / pro - duce: o/pdu o/pdc

	SC	OV
over/consume	___	___
counter/propose	___	___
over/develop	___	___

Suffix Compound

Example: headlines > head - lin - es : h/lis h/lns

	SC	OV
north/easterly	___	___
over/balance	___	___
land/owner	___	___
easy/going	___	___
ware/house	___	___
score/keeper	___	___
out/rageous	___	___
noise/maker	___	___
electro/magnetism	___	___

Prefix/Suffix Compound

Example: counterproposal > counter / pro – pos - al: c/ppl

	SC
over/confidence	___
over/development	___
over/extension	___
over/exposing	___

NOTES

Studying MiniScript Symbol Forms

Study and memorize the alphabetical abbreviations and symbol forms below:

bath/room	b/ro	b/rm		
court/yard	c/ya	c/yd		
girl/friend	g/fr			
electro/therapy	e/th			
boy/friend	b/fr			
main/stream	m/st			
down/turn	d/tu	d/tn		
down/hill	d/hi	d/hl		
bench/mark	b/ma	b/mk		
class/room	c/ro	c/rm		
water/front	w/fr			
flash/light	f/li	f/lt		
over/extend	o/xte	o/xtd		
over/protect	o/pte	o/ptt		
over/develop	o/dve	o/dvp		
north/easterly	n/eay	n/esy		
there/fore	t/fo	t/fr		
chair/man	c/ma	c/mn		
over/balance	o/bac	o/blc		
land/owner	l/owr			
easy/going	e/gog			

60

NOTES

word	form 1	form 2		
ware/house	**w/ho**	**w/hs**	^/ ‘ <	^/ ‘
score/keeper	**s/ker**	**s/kpr**	–/ >’)	–/ >)
out/rageous	**o/ras**	**o/rgs**	•– </)	‘– </)
noise/maker	**n/mar**	**n/mkr**	<• </)	<• </–>)
electro/magnetism	**e/mam**	**e/mgm**	<• ’/ <	<‘ ’/ <
counter/proposal	**c/ppl**		)) •/ >	
over/confidence	**o/cfc**		</•·••	
over/development	**o/dvm**		’^< </	
over/extension	**o/xth**		–‘ </^	
over/exposing	**o/xpg**		)‘ </^	

Practicing MiniScript Symbol Forms

Write the appropriate symbols forms for the words below:

bath/room

court/yard

girl/friend

electro/therapy

boy/friend

main/stream

down/turn

down/hill

bench/mark

NOTES

class/room

water/front

flash/light

over/extend

over/protect

over/develop

north/easterly

there/fore

chair/man

over/balance

land/owner

easy/going

ware/house

score/keeper

out/rageous

noise/maker

electro/magnetism

counter/proposal

over/confidence

over/development

over/extension

over/exposing

NOTES